TO:
_____

FROM:
_____

DATE:
_____

The Adventures of Super Obi: Nothing to Fear

Published by Okonkwo Press, LLC

Copyright © 2021 by Dominique Okonkwo

All rights reserved. No part of this book may be reproduced or transmitted in any form or by any means, electronic or mechanical, including photocopying, recording, or by any information storage and retrieval system, without written permission from the author.

For information, address the author online at www.dominiqueokonkwo.com

Scripture quotations are taken from the Holy Bible, New Living Translation, copyright ©1996, 2004, 2015 by Tyndale House Foundation. Used by permission of Tyndale House Publishers, Carol Stream, Illinois 60188. All rights reserved.

ISBN 978-1-7373823-0-0 (Hardback)
ISBN 978-1-7373823-1-7 (Paperback)
ISBN 978-1-7373823-2-4 (Digital Online)

Library of Congress Cataloging-in-Publication Data

Names:	Okonkwo, Dominique, 1984- author.	Hnatenko, Mariana, illustrator.
Title:	The adventures of Super Obi : nothing to fear / Dominique Okonkwo; illustrated by Mariana Hnatenko.
Other titles:	Nothing to fear.
Description:	First edition.	Miami : Okonkwo Press, [2021]	Series: The adventures of Super Obi ; 1.	Audience: ages 2-8.	Summary: Obi has just been tucked into bed by his mother for the night, only to find himself face-to-face with his fears... or is he? This book is a fun, super bedtime adventure for the whole family that includes a short quiet time and prayer time at the end of the story.--Publisher.
Identifiers:	ISBN: 978-1-7373823-0-0 (Hardback)	978-1-7373823-1-7 (Paperback)	978-1-7373823-2-4 (Digital Online)	LCCN: 2021911826
Subjects:	LCSH: Bedtime--Juvenile fiction.	Fear--Juvenile fiction.	Monsters--Juvenile fiction.	Mother and child--Juvenile fiction.	Father and child--Juvenile fiction.	Courage--Juvenile fiction.	Individuality--Juvenile fiction.	God (Christianity)--Love--Juvenile fiction.	Christian life-- Juvenile fiction.	Bedtime prayers.	Children's stories.	CYAC: Bedtime--Fiction.	Fear-- Fiction.	Monsters--Fiction.	Mother and child--Fiction.	Father and child--Fiction.	Courage --Fiction.	Individuality--Fiction.	God (Christianity)--Love--Fiction.	Christian life.	Bedtime prayers.	LCGFT: Prayers.	Christian fiction.	Devotional literature.
Classification:	LCC: PZ7.1.O448 N68 2021	DDC: [E]--dc23

Illustrated by Mariana Hnatenko
Developmental Edit by Brooke Vitale

Printed in the United States
First Edition, November 2021

"Let the children come to me.
Don't stop them! For the Kingdom of God belongs
to those who are like these children."

— Mark 10:14 (NLT)

For Obinna, Adanna, and Amara

— D.O.

"Good night, Mommy," Obi said as his mother tucked him snugly into his bed.

Mommy smiled and gave him a big kiss on the forehead. "Good night, Obi," she said.

Obi rolled over and got comfortable. As he started to close his eyes, he realized . . . Mommy had forgotten to turn on his night-light!

"Mommy," Obi whispered.

But it was too late. Mommy was gone.

The moonlight crept through Obi's window, making everything look mysterious. Suddenly, Obi noticed a flicker of light deep inside his closet. Panicked, he squeezed his trusty blankie tight. He was convinced the light must be the gleaming eyes of a monster hiding in the closet.

Downstairs, Obi heard a loud
BANG, CHANG-A-LANG, CHANG.

Leaping out of bed, Obi raced to his bedroom door. He swung it open, coming face-to-face with the dark hallway.

"Mommy!" he yelled. "What was that noise?"

But there was no answer.

The house was now quiet, dark, and *very spooky*.

The shadows around Obi started to grow, moving closer.
They're coming for me! Obi realized. *I need to hide!*

Determined to find a safe space, Obi slammed his door shut and dove under his covers.

He squeezed his eyes tight, hoping that whatever was out there wouldn't find him.

Then Obi heard it: a faint *thump* downstairs.

Curious, he opened his right eye.

Slowly, the thumping noise got louder and LOUDER. With each *thump*, the sound moved closer to his room.

Obi's eyes got bigger and BIGGER. He'd never heard anything so loud in his life!

There must be a giant in the house, and he is coming to GET ME!

"Momm—" Obi started to yell, but he stopped when he heard his bedroom door slowly creak open.

Obi held his breath, trying his best not to make a sound.
But it seemed the giant knew where he was.
The ground shook with each step the giant took toward Obi's bed.

"Obi," called the giant. "Oh, Obi . . ."

Obi listened to the voice. *Wait a minute,* he thought. *That giant sounds like . . .*

Obi threw back his covers. "Daddy!"

"Are you okay, Obi?" Daddy said. "I heard you screaming for Mommy."

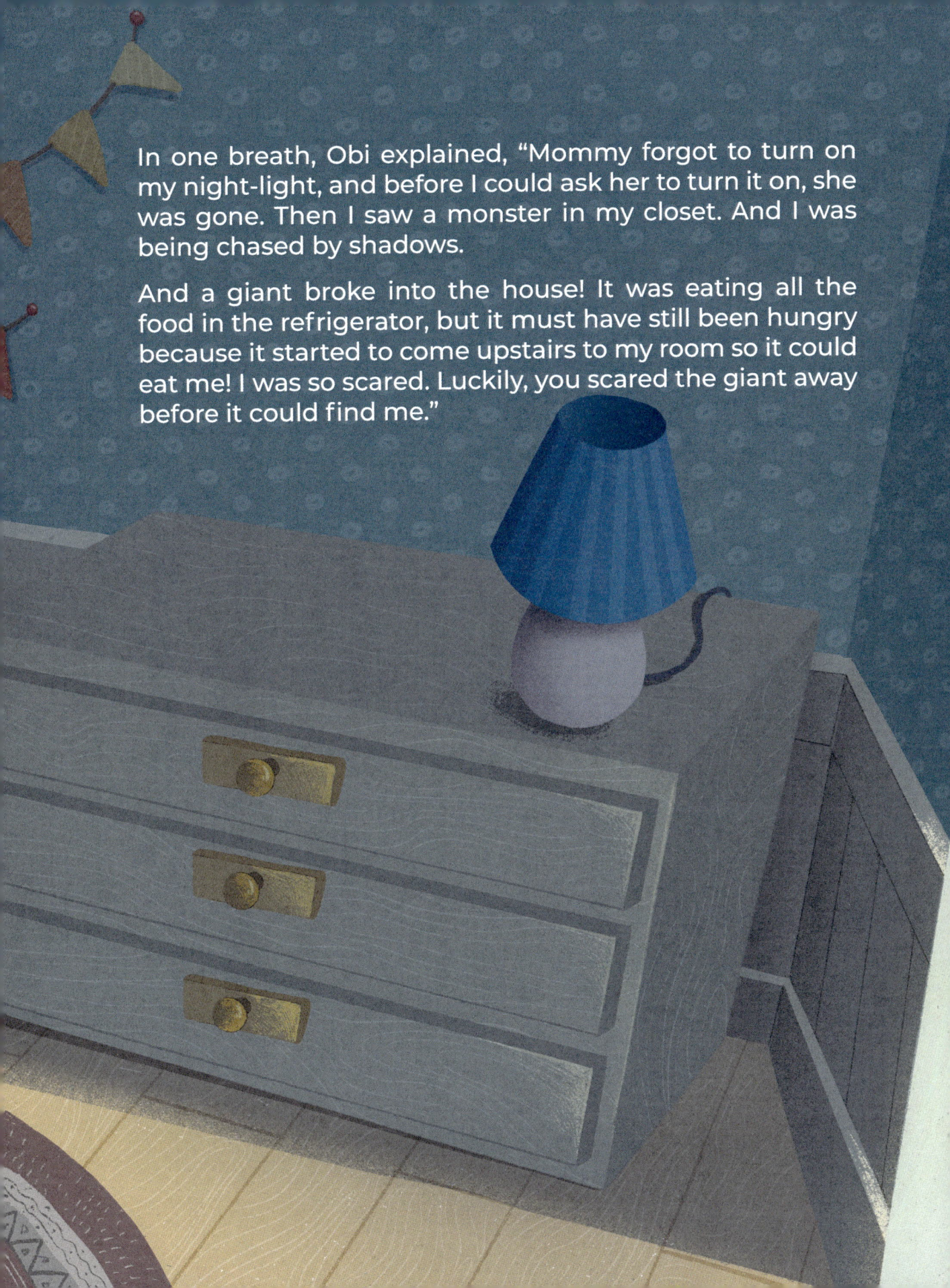

In one breath, Obi explained, "Mommy forgot to turn on my night-light, and before I could ask her to turn it on, she was gone. Then I saw a monster in my closet. And I was being chased by shadows.

And a giant broke into the house! It was eating all the food in the refrigerator, but it must have still been hungry because it started to come upstairs to my room so it could eat me! I was so scared. Luckily, you scared the giant away before it could find me."

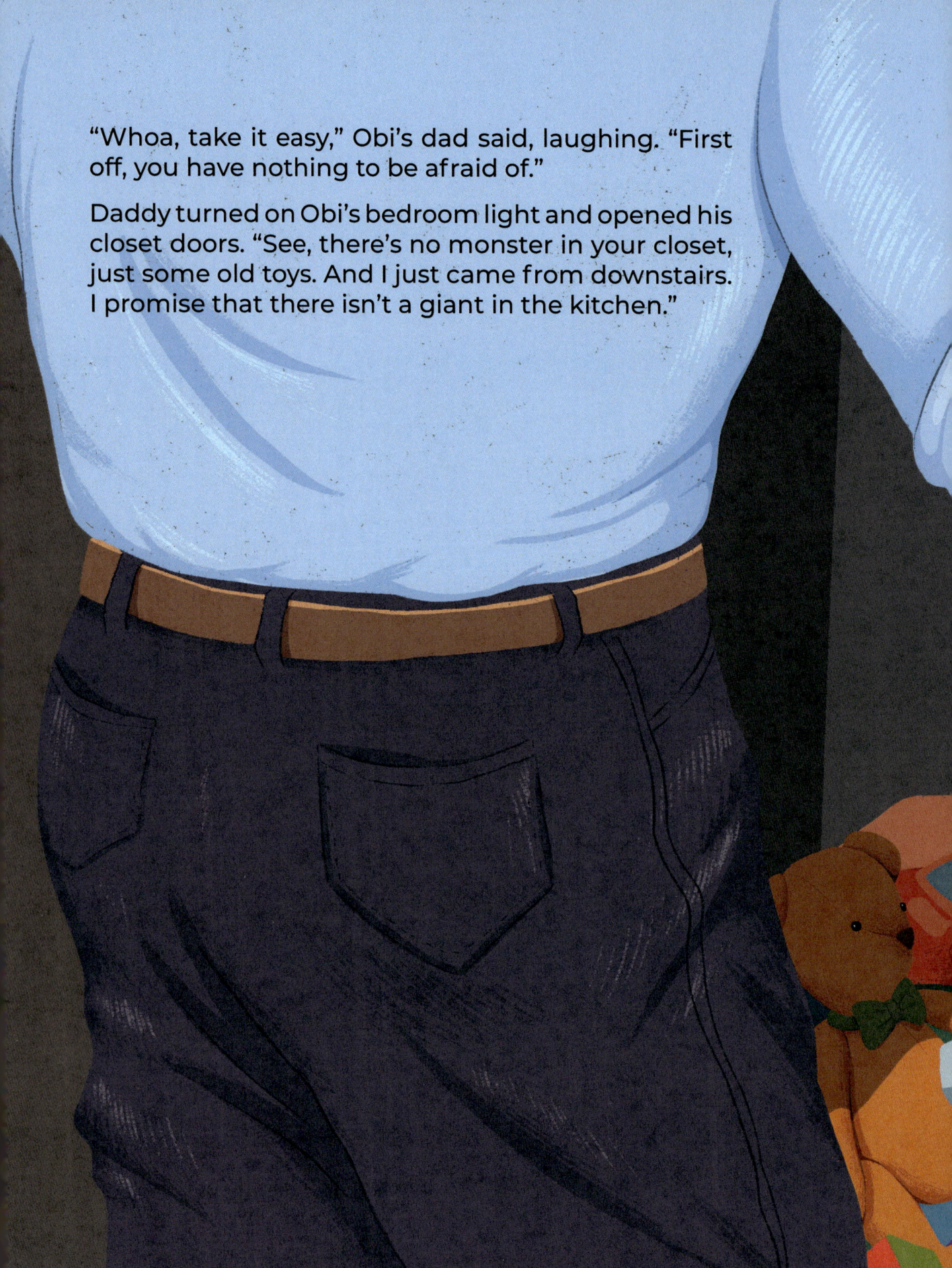

"Whoa, take it easy," Obi's dad said, laughing. "First off, you have nothing to be afraid of."

Daddy turned on Obi's bedroom light and opened his closet doors. "See, there's no monster in your closet, just some old toys. And I just came from downstairs. I promise that there isn't a giant in the kitchen."

Obi peered into the closet. No monster.

He carefully looked around his room. No giant and no shadows.

"See, nothing to fear," Daddy said. "Everything you thought you saw was just your imagination."

"My imagination?" Obi asked.

"That's right," Daddy said. "But you know what? I'm proud of you. Even though you were scared, you were super brave! And if you ask me, that makes you pretty special."

Obi smiled and sighed in relief. "I am special. And super," said Obi. "Super Obi—that's me!"

Daddy tucked Obi into bed and gave him a kiss good night. Then, with a wink, he turned on Obi's night-light.

"Good night, Super Obi," he said as he closed the door.

"Good night, Daddy," Obi whispered. Then, wrapped in his blankie, Obi yawned and began to slip into a peaceful night's sleep.

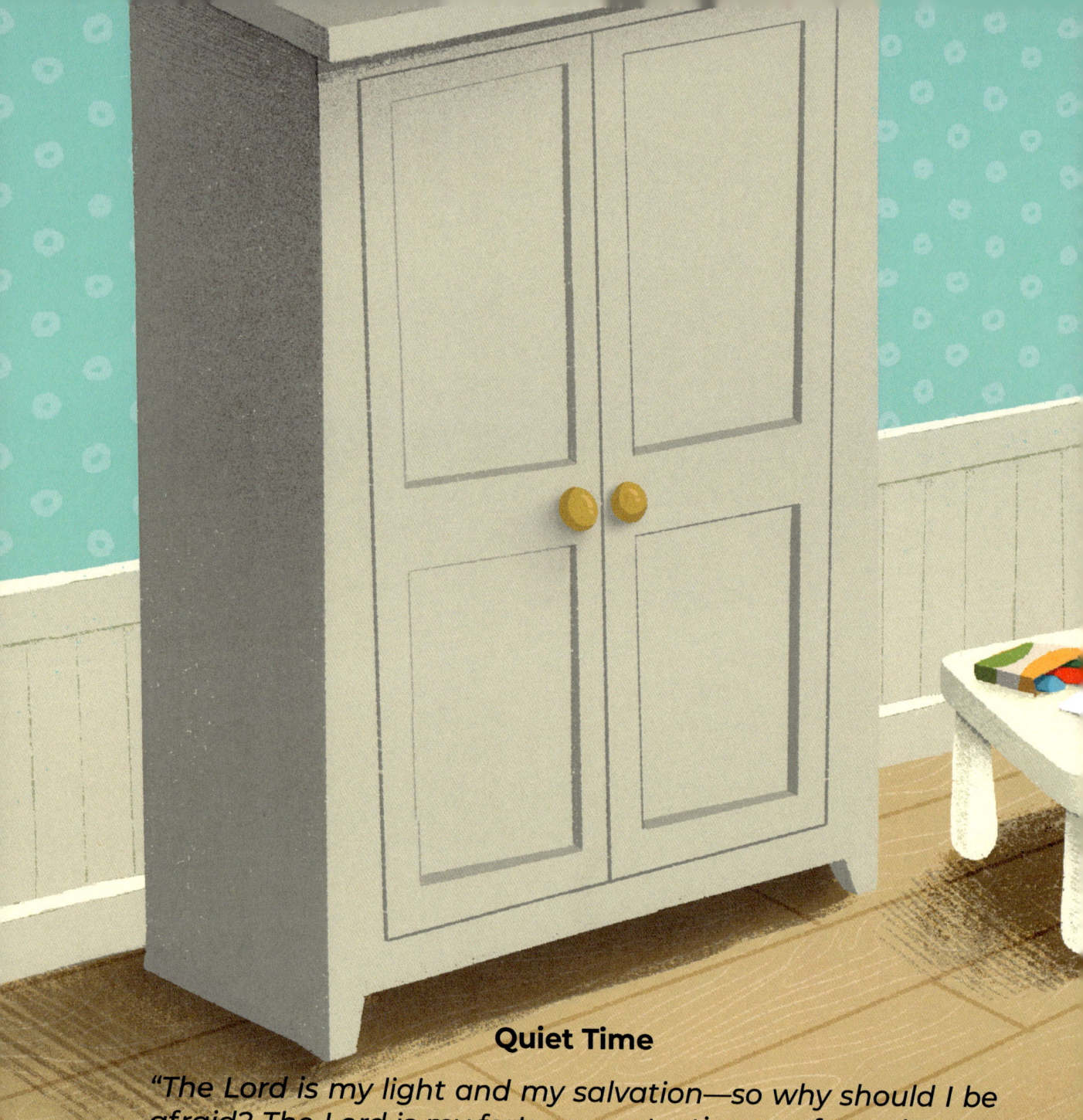

Quiet Time

"The Lord is my light and my salvation—so why should I be afraid? The Lord is my fortress, protecting me from danger, so why should I tremble?"

— Psalm 27:1 (NLT)

Do you ever feel afraid? Do you ever feel like you are in danger? Who do you turn to when you need help? Remember that God is always there to provide us with help and support, because we are all His children. Just like our parents do, He wants us to feel His love and protection.

Prayer Time

"Dear God,

Thank you for being a God of courage and strength. You have made strong many of your children, like Moses, David, and your son Jesus Christ. May we remember that you hope for us to work through our fears and know we aren't alone.

Amen."

Dear Readers,

Who is Obi, and why is he so super? Are not all children his age with the imagination to be and do anything they put their minds to super? I created The Adventures of Super Obi to celebrate that all children are super in their own ways. In this story, Obi is a kid who has a nuclear family and a trusty blankie that gives him the courage to face any obstacle, including those he creates.

Super Obi is modeled after my firstborn son, Obinna Okonkwo. I am Haitian-American and Obi's father is Nigerian. I also have two other children with loads of personality. I have been on many adventures with my kids. My son and all our wild family adventures are the inspiration for this book. As a young child, Obinna carried his yellow blankie with him for comfort and courage.

Obi's blankie, when tied around his neck as a cape, gives him the strength and courage to conquer his fears and anxieties. I believe many children still have those security objects for emotional support during their early adolescent years. To all the children reading this book, just remember that you, too, are super, no matter your fears, and that God, like a warm blankie, is always there to surround you with love and to give you strength.

I'd love to hear from you! Be sure to visit me online at dominiqueokonkwo.com and subscribe today to get notified about the next Super Obi Adventure—and get access to FREE downloads like Super Obi coloring and activity pages!

Like this book? Please leave a review on Amazon and share this book on social media with the hashtag #SuperObiBook. I can be found @miamimotherhood on Instagram. I truly appreciate you!

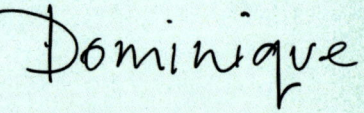

Dominique (left) with her family Obinna, Adanna, Louis, and Amara (in that order)

Obinna at age 3

Made in the USA
Columbia, SC
08 July 2022